T. S. ELIOT

With many thanks to Tom Rayner

T.S. ELIOT

Sue Asbee

The Rourke Corporation, Inc.
Vero Beach, FL 32964

Life and Works

The Brontës
Joseph Conrad
Charles Dickens
T. S. Eliot
Hemingway
D. H. Lawrence
Katherine Mansfield
George Orwell
Shakespeare
John Steinbeck
H. G. Wells
Virginia Woolf

Cover illustration by David Armitage

Text © 1990 The Rourke Corporation, Inc.

Library of Congress Cataloging–in–Publication Data
Asbee, Sue.
    T. S. Eliot / by Sue Asbee.
      p. cm. — (Life and works)
    Includes bibliographical references.
    Summary: Briefly surveys the life of the modern American poet and analyzes in depth some of his major works.
    ISBN 0–86593–022–8
    1. Eliot, T. S. (Thomas Stearns), 1888–1965—Juvenile literature. 2. Poets, American—20th century—Biography—Juvenile literature. [1. Eliot, T. S. (Thomas Stearns), 1888–1965—Criticism and interpretation. 2. American literature—History and criticism.]
    I. Title. II. Series.
PS3509.L43Z8244 1990
821'.912—dc20
[B]
                                     90–8213
                                         CIP
                                         AC

Contents

1 The Life of T. S. Eliot

In my own experience of the appreciation of poetry I have always found that the less I know about the poet and his work, before I begin to read it, the better. A quotation, a critical remark, an enthusiastic essay, may well be the accident that sets one to reading a particular author; but an elaborate preparation of historical and biographical knowledge has always been to me a barrier . . . it is better to be spurred to acquire the scholarship because you enjoy the poetry, than to suppose that you enjoy the poetry because you have acquired the scholarship.

(from T.S.Eliot's essay on Dante)

T. S. Eliot was not happy about the prospect of a biography. He was an intensely private man with strong views on "impersonality" in poetry. He was influential in shaping the way in which English literature has come to be studied in the twentieth century, believing in careful study of the words on the page. Any illumination that knowledge of a writer's personal life might shed on his or her work he considered more or less irrelevant.

Eliot was an important critic, as well as poet and dramatist; by the end of his life he had become a public figure. In 1956 14,000 people filled a baseball stadium at the University of Minnesota in Minneapolis to hear him lecture on "The Frontiers of Criticism." Such was his fame that many came to see him in the flesh as much as to hear his talk.

Opposite *Portrait of T.S. Eliot by his contemporary, Percy Wyndham Lewis.*

Thomas Stearns Eliot was born on September 26, 1888 in St. Louis, Missouri, the youngest of six children. His father, Henry Ware Eliot, was a successful and wealthy businessman who, in his youth, wanted to be a painter. His mother, Charlotte, whose maiden name was Stearns, was a teacher until her marriage. She wrote poems, which occasionally she sent to newspapers, but considered herself to be a failure and recognized very early that her son's talent outshone her own.

Eliot aged about twelve on the links with his father, Henry Ware Eliot.

The Eliot family spent each summer in New England and, eventually, in 1896, had a house built at Eastern Point in Gloucester, which overlooked the harbor, the Atlantic Ocean and the rocks known as the Dry Salvages. (Eliot was to remember these and use them in one of his *Four Quartets* over forty years later.) He had always been a delicate child; nevertheless, he took great pleasure in sailing. The ocean and the great Mississippi River, which he could hear from his home in St. Louis, acted upon his imagination.

9

The house at Eastern Point, New England, where Eliot spent summer vacations as a child.

His poem "The Dry Salvages" opens with a description of the river, its "rhythm present in the nursery bedroom." In later life he wrote that "there is something in having passed one's childhood beside the big river which is incommunicable to those who have not."

When he was ten, he began studying French and German, ancient history, Greek and Latin at Smith Academy in St. Louis. He worked hard and, perhaps partly because of his poor health, which did not allow him to take part in sports, he was a naturally "bookish" child. His interest in writing also developed early: he produced eight issues of his own magazine called *The Fireside*, which consisted of "Fiction, Gossip, Theater and Jokes." At school he studied Milton and Browning; other poets, such as Henry King, he discovered for himself. Perhaps more importantly, he showed an early talent for imitating the styles of other writers.

Smith Academy in St. Louis where Eliot first went to school.

Eliot was awarded the Latin prize before he left Smith Academy, and he could have gone straight to Harvard University in 1905. Although he was educationally advanced, he had not enjoyed much companionship with people of his own age, and his parents decided he should have a year at Milton Academy, near Boston. In later years he remembered the experience of leaving home as an uncertain and not entirely happy one. Removed from the protective wing of his family, and the reflected status that their position in St. Louis society conferred on him, he became self-conscious. One of the first things he noticed was his own drawling accent, which seemed out of place in Boston, and he quickly modified it.

In 1906 Eliot went to Harvard University. Seven years later, after postgraduate study, he became a teaching assistant in the Department of Philosophy.

In 1906 he went to Harvard University and decided to complete his degree in three years instead of the more usual four, so that he could work for a master's degree in English during the fourth year. It is from this period that his earliest poetry dates, although it did not appear for many years. "Portrait of a Lady" was begun not long after Eliot discovered Arthur Symon's book *The Symbolist Movement in Literature*. Eliot's poem is about the

Opposite *In 1910
Eliot went to study
at the Sorbonne in
Paris.*

contradiction between polite social occasions – such as having tea with friends – and underlying feelings of desperation, which good manners decree must never be voiced.

In his postgraduate year Eliot was taught by Irving Babbitt, a distinguished man whose lectures had more influence on Eliot than any others he attended at Harvard. Through Babbitt, he became interested in Sanskrit and Buddhism – both of which surfaced many years later in *The Waste Land*. Babbitt stressed the importance of discipline and some kind of guiding authority. This struck a chord with Eliot's own feelings; much of his early poetry, up to and including *The Waste Land*, presents images of a society bewildered and adrift because it lacks any guiding belief.

Eliot's family were Unitarians, but he had rejected that background and was not at that time searching for any particular faith. Nevertheless, the sense of failure and confusion expressed in his poetry can be partly attributed to his rejection of any guiding principles. The first two poems in the sequence that is now known as "Preludes" were written by the summer of 1910.

Eliot's own manners and appearance were always impeccably corrrect. But he was stifled by the routine of bourgeois life in Boston even while he was a part of it. His reading, as always, was wide, but his interest in the poet Jules Laforgue, his reading of Baudelaire, and the fact that his chosen course of study was literary criticism in France, all prompted him to go to Paris in 1910. He studied French literature at the Sorbonne and attended Henri Bergson's lectures at the College de France. Bergson was a philosopher whose ideas – which included ideas on the nature of time – were widely read and influential. The modernist writers James Joyce and Virginia Woolf expressed similar ideas: that one has an intuitive sense of time, in one's mind and memory, that does not necessarily agree with standard "clock time." This conflict between "inner" and "outer" time is apparent in Eliot's poem "Rhapsody on a Windy Night."

Eliot visited London and Munich during this trip to Europe. He then returned to Harvard for the next three years, partly in response to family and financial pressures. He studied Sanskrit and Indian philosophy, and became very interested in F.H. Bradley's philosophy when he read

the book *Appearance and Reality*. By 1913, Eliot was a teaching assistant in the Department of Philosophy, and the following year he was offered a scholarship that enabled him to travel and study at Merton College, Oxford. His thesis on F. H. Bradley's philosophy was completed in 1917.

The poet Conrad Aiken, a friend from Harvard, was already living in London when Eliot arrived and introduced him to many leading literary figures. The man who became an even more invaluable help to him was another American based in London, the poet Ezra Pound. He was not much older than Eliot, but he had published

Merton College, Oxford. Eliot was awarded a scholarship that allowed him to study at Oxford University in 1914.

several volumes of his own poetry and had contacts and influence. Through Pound, Eliot met Wyndham Lewis, who edited a literary magazine called *Blast*, in which Eliot's "Preludes" and "Rhapsody on a Windy Night" were first published. Through the philosopher Bertrand Russell, whom he had met at Harvard, he met Lady Ottoline Morrell, a self-appointed patroness of the arts who was friendly with writers such as D.H.Lawrence, Aldous Huxley, Katherine Mansfield and Virginia and Leonard Woolf. The most important aspect of this new circle of aquaintances was that they all took art and literature very seriously.

Ezra Pound. Like Eliot, Pound was an American living and working in London.

He went up to Oxford in 1914. In 1915 he met and married Vivien Haigh-Wood, a young Englishwoman from an upper-middle-class background. From that moment it was necessary for him to earn a living; first by schoolteaching, later by working at Lloyds Bank in the City of London.

Lady Ottoline Morrell, who was friendly with some of the leading artists of the day.

His first marriage was not particularly happy, as both he and his wife were of a nervous disposition and uncertain health. Eliot was frequently ill and, as the years went by, unhappy with his private life. But he preserved appearances as much as he was able, and his poetry can be considered in this light. "The Love Song of J.Alfred Prufrock" and "Portrait of a Lady" pre-date his marriage, and show an awareness of the discrepancy between inner feelings that may be difficult – if not impossible – to express and the outer forms of day-to-day behavior that must be preserved. The poems are an attempt to reconcile a sense of inner confusion with an ordered outer life. Order, of a kind, is displayed through life's daily routines – going to work, coming home, passing the time in trivial occupations. These activities are shown, in one way or another, to be necessary to sustain existence, but often mask an internal sense of frustration. Through the organization of the poetry, however, a different order emerges, which allows both of these realities to be expressed.

The image that Eliot presented to the world was one of a reserved gentleman, scrupulous in his observation of social niceties. In spite of this, he did not feel he really belonged in English society, any more than he felt at home in the U.S. He thought of himself in England as a resident alien. His first volume of poetry, *Prufrock and Other Observations*, was published in 1917, shortly after he started work at Lloyds Bank, largely as a result of Ezra Pound's efforts on his behalf. At the same time he accepted the job of assistant editor on the literary journal the *Egoist*, which brought in a modest sum of money and increased his workload considerably. He gave a series of lectures on Victorian literature, which again were time-consuming and brought little financial return. For a while he felt as though he would never have time to write poetry again.

Wyndham Lewis pointed out that as soon as he had settled "on this side of the water" Eliot was entertained with "the spectacle of Europe committing suicide" (a reference to the First World War, 1914–18). He did not write directly about the War, but one way of looking at his great poem *The Waste Land* is to remember the destruction of lives caused by the War and the fact that London itself seemed like a wasteland. Eliot himself was unfit for military service for medical reasons.

The Waste Land began life as a series of verse fragments. It was originally considerably longer than its final published state, and the working title was "He Do the Police in Different Voices," a quotation from Dickens's Our Mutual Friend. Eliot was working closely with Pound on various literary ventures and sent him what became The Waste Land for his comments. Pound adopted the role of editor, and Eliot almost always accepted his suggestions. The fourth section, "Death by Water," was originally much longer and included descriptions of a voyage on a sailing ship. Pound pared it down to eight lines dealing with the

Opposite *Eliot in 1919.*

Virginia Woolf. References to Eliot can be found in her diaries; when she writes of "Tom just coming upstairs for tea" he sounds reassuringly ordinary and unpoetic.

23

death by drowning of Phlebas, the Phoenician sailor. Pound also advised against including the poem "Gerontion" as a preface to *The Waste Land* and suggested he cut a long section that would have preceded "April is the cruellest month," the present opening of the poem. The original manuscripts were found and published after Eliot's death, clearly showing some of Pound's comments and suggestions, and those of Vivien Eliot, in the margins. Pound's editorial skills undoubtedly pulled the poem into its final shape.

The Waste Land was published in *Criterion*, a literary magazine Eliot edited, in October 1922. It came out in book form in September of the following year, published by Virginia and Leonard Woolf's Hogarth Press. Critical comment was varied when it first appeared. One reviewer described it as a "mad medley," and although he did not intend to be complimentary (it is "so much waste paper," he concluded), the remark has some truth. Eliot set down in the poem his vision of the modern consciousness, which certainly he did not see as sane.

Eliot had frequently used references to other literary works in his earlier poetry, and when the Woolfs published his poem he added explanatory notes at the end. The notes are there partly to refute charges of plagiarism – we are fully intended to recognize his sources – but also, they allow Eliot's sense of humor to emerge at the expense of earnest literary scholarship. He cites some, but certainly not all, of his sources; others are quite unnecessary: the lines "the hermit-thrush sings in the pine trees / Drip drop drip drop drop drop drop" have a footnote citing a book of North American birds!

In 1925 Eliot left Lloyds Bank to work in the more congenial surroundings of Faber and Gwyer, the publishing house that has since become Faber and Faber. Over the years he was instrumental in recognizing and promoting other poets. He published Stephen Spender and Louis MacNeice's work, James Joyce's *Finnegan's Wake,* and eventually poets such as Ted Hughes and Thom Gunn.

Two years after leaving the bank, Eliot joined the Anglican Church. This was an important turning point in his life, and it had equally important implications for his poetry. "Ash Wednesday" and "The Journey of the Magi" belong to this period. In 1927, he became a British citizen.

By the 1930s his reputation was established. He gave a number of radio broadcasts, and in 1932 accepted the Charles Eliot Norton visiting professorship at Harvard. A series of lectures that he gave there was later published as *The Uses of Poetry and the Uses of Criticism*. His wife remained in England while he was in Boston, and they never lived together again. She died in 1947. Ten years later he married a young woman named Valerie Fletcher, who had been his secretary. His second marriage provided happiness and contentment in his later years.

In 1934, Eliot was asked to write a pageant in order to raise money for a number of London churches. The result was *The Rock*, which contains the chilling lines:

> The desert is not remote in southern tropics,
> The desert is not only around the corner,
> The desert is squeezed in the tube-train next to you,
> The desert is in the heart of your brother.

Deserts and tube trains recall the imagery of *The Waste Land*, but the whole spirit is different here. *The Rock* led to *Murder in the Cathedral*, a historical verse drama written for Canterbury Cathedral about the murder of Thomas à Becket. It was a tremendous success. It transferred from the Cathedral to London, and thereafter to provincial theaters – although that had not been the original intention. Certain lines were cut from the play because they were not strictly necessary to the action. These became the basis for Eliot's next major poem, "Burnt Norton."

He had visited Burnt Norton, a house near Chipping Campden in Gloucestershire, in 1934. It is not an important stately home, but the visit had private significance for him. The poem "East Coker" evolved in much the same way. Eliot first visited the Somerset village because his family had lived there 200 years earlier; his ancestor Andrew Eliot settled in America in the late seventeenth century. It was while working on "East Coker" that he decided to compose a sequence of poems – "The Dry Salvages" (1941), and the last of the *Four Quartets*, "Little Gidding," in 1943. If "The Dry Salvages" was inspired by childhood memories, "Little Gidding" invoked the present day. The difficulties of London life during the war-time blitz (Eliot served as a fire watcher) affected his concentration, and he found it difficult to work on the poem.

Opposite *A London audience lining up to see the hugely popular Eliot play* The Cocktail Party.

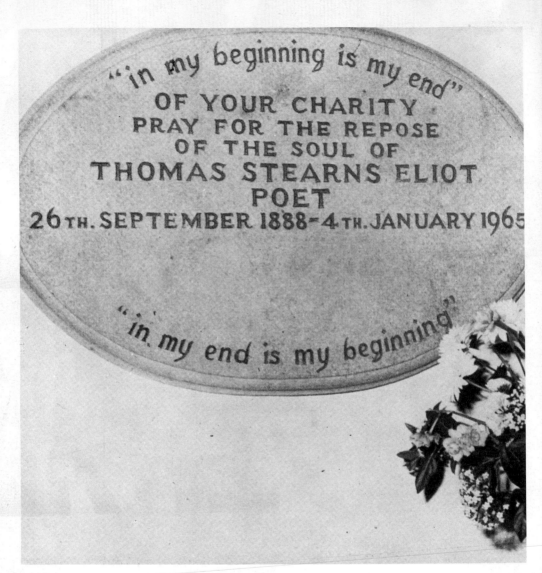

"in my beginning is my end"
OF YOUR CHARITY
PRAY FOR THE REPOSE
OF THE SOUL OF
THOMAS STEARNS ELIOT
POET
26TH. SEPTEMBER 1888–4TH. JANUARY 1965
"in my end is my beginning"

The Eliot memorial in St. Michael's Church, East Coker.

Opposite *Eliot receiving the Nobel Prize for Literature in Stockholm, 1948.*

He wrote four more plays after *Murder in the Cathedral*: *The Family Reunion* was performed first in 1939, *The Cocktail Party* nearly eight years later. *The Confidential Clerk* and *The Elder Statesman* belong to the 1950s.

Eliot's work in the service of literature was officially recognized when he won the Nobel Prize in 1948; in the same year he was awarded the Order of Merit by King George VI. After periods in the hospital he died at home on January 4, 1965. His ashes were taken to the church at East Coker, the home of his ancestors.

2 The Early Poems

I liked him, though I may say not at all connecting him with texts Ezra had shown me about some fictional character dreadfully troubled with old age, in which the lines (for it had been verse) "I am old, I am growing old, I shall wear the bottoms of my trousers rolled" feature . . . I was unable to make head or tail of . . .

(Wyndham Lewis on T.S.Eliot)

Wyndham Lewis was not alone in his inability to make sense of Eliot's early poetry. Rupert Brooke had shown "Prufrock" to Harold Monroe, the influential owner of the Poetry Bookshop, who felt that it was "absolutely insane." These reactions were not surprising, for the poems were quite unlike any written in English before. They appeared "difficult" because they were new, not because Eliot wished to be obscure or create puzzles for readers to solve. His writing was complex because his perception of the world was not simple or straightforward. Poems celebrating love or the beauties of nature no longer seemed appropriate, nor did the regular rhymes and verse that the Victorian poets had used. Eliot continued to use both meter and rhyme, but in his own particular way, so that breaks or discordancies are as important as regularities. He thought hard about the world he described, and readers have to do their share of thinking. Eliot never provides easy answers, but instead asks demanding questions: it is here that the interest of his poetry lies.

Opposite Rupert Brooke, 1887 – 1915. *Brooke's own poetry was very different from Eliot's, but he helped draw attention to Eliot's early work.*

The poems published in *Prufrock and Other Observations* (1917) were all written in the U.S. and belong to Eliot's Harvard years. It is unlikely that he asked "what is the self?" and "what is reality?" when he wrote "The Love Song of J. Alfred Prufrock," "Portrait of a Lady," "Rhapsody on a Windy Night," "Preludes" and "Hysteria," but such questions make good starting points for understanding his poems. While at Harvard he studied philosophy, in particular F. H. Bradley's work on appearance and reality, concepts that were the source of much of his poetry. The most important question he asks is, what is the relationship between the self and outside reality? Do we simply observe the world around us, or are we an integral part of it? One approach to the complexities of these questions is to think of newborn babies, who, it is believed, are unable to distinguish between where their bodies end and their surroundings begin. At what point of our development, then, do we become aware that our parents, or perhaps the sides of our cot, are not simply extensions of ourselves? Or is the idea that we are each self-contained, separate entities equally false? There are, of course, no straightforward answers, but these are some of the questions posed by Eliot in his early work.

Opposite *Portrait of the poet as a youth.*

Polite social gatherings are often seen as a way of avoiding more important issues in Eliot's poetry. "And would it have been worth it, after all, / After the cups, the marmalade, the tea . . . To have squeezed the universe into a ball / To roll it to some overwhelming question . . . " ("Prufrock").

Eliot never speaks directly to the reader; poetry, he said, "is not the expression of personality, but an escape from personality." Most of the poems are dramatic monologues. He invents fictional personalities – like Prufrock, or the young man in "Portrait of a Lady" – and it is their voices that speak, rather than his own. Unlike the invented personas of the nineteenth-century poet Browning's dramatic monologues, Eliot's characters are shifting and unstable. It is difficult, if not impossible, to imagine a context for them: often we learn little of their background.

The most extreme example of this is the short prose poem "Hysteria." There is no narrative voice to explain the context to us. All that we learn about the speaker has to be inferred by listening to what the voice says. Indeed, there is no real evidence to indicate gender; it is likely to be male, but that conclusion can be reached only if we agree that the fear of being swallowed and consumed by a woman is an indication of this particular individual's masculine sexual anxiety.

> As she laughed I was aware of becoming involved in her laughter and being part of it, until her teeth were only accidental stars with a talent for squad-drill. I was drawn in by short gasps, inhaled at each momentary recovery, lost finally in the dark caverns of her throat, bruised by the ripple of unseen muscles. An elderly waiter with trembling hands was hurriedly spreading a pink and white checked table cloth over the rusty green iron table, saying: "If the lady and gentleman wish to take their tea in the garden, if the lady and gentleman wish to take their tea in the garden . . ." I decided that if the shaking of her breasts could be stopped, some of the fragments of the afternoon might be collected, and I concentrated my attention with careful subtlety to this end.

("Hysteria")

The situation is very simple. Someone watches a woman laughing, and a waiter suggests that a lady and gentleman go into a garden for tea. To understand why that is sufficiently interesting to write about, we need to ask a number of questions. Is the waiter addressing the speaker and his companion or two quite separate individuals? Is the woman who is laughing the speaker's companion or merely someone he sees? Why does he feel absorbed by

34

her laughter, and why choose such bizarre images to describe it? We have no way of finding out. If we ask whether another observer would describe the scene in the same way, however, it becomes apparent that that is precisely where the interest lies: in the speaker's very unusual perceptions and consciousness.

The first few words describe a fairly common occurrence: "as she laughed I was aware of becoming involved in her laughter." Most people could testify to laughter being infectious, but as the sentence continues it becomes more extraordinary, so that our first

A tea garden in 1909. The idea of characters losing their grip becomes more scandalous when it takes place in a social setting like this one, as we see in Eliot's prose poem "Hysteria."

understanding of it has to be questioned. What might have been considered a figure of speech – "and being part of it" – is intended quite literally by the speaker:

> . . . I was drawn in by short gasps, inhaled at each momentary recovery, lost finally in the dark caverns of her throat, bruised by the ripple of unseen muscles.

The experience is not one of shared merriment, but of loss of identity. "Drawn in," "inhaled," "lost," and "bruised" are very physical expressions, ordinary in themselves, but not usually used to describe mental states. Who, then, is

Dancing and drinking at the Trocadero in 1921. "And I have known the arms already, known them all – / Arms that are braceleted and white and bare / (But in the lamplight downed with light brown hair!)" ("Prufrock").

hysterical? The laughing woman, or the person who describes his response to the laughter? We do not know much about the woman, but the speaker has so little sense of himself as a separate individual, that by talking about what he sees, he describes his own crisis of identity. What is observed becomes an indication of a state of mind. Eliot described this when he wrote of F.H. Bradley's beliefs: "I, the objective world, and my feelings about it, are an indissoluble whole."

The passage about the waiter in the middle of "Hysteria" can be read as an attempt to hold on to external reality, but

there are too many descriptive words, so they simply reinforce the unstable mental state: "An *elderly* waiter with *trembling* hands was *hurriedly* spreading a *pink* and *white checked* cloth over the *rusty iron green* table" (added emphasis). In displaying his powers of observation in order to reassure himself that he is separate, he presents too much detail, with the result that there is no sense of normality.

The waiter himself, with his mechanical repetition of "if the lady and gentleman wish to take their tea in the garden" sounds, from the way he is reported, as if he too might be on the verge of madness; and it is no accident that the speaker picks up the same rhythm and construction when he stops reporting the waiter's words: "I decided that *if the shaking* . . ." If he felt drawn in by the woman's laughter, he has unconsciously absorbed the waiter's speech pattern. Where, then, does the speaker's sense of separateness, or individuality, lie? In a calmly sinister manner, he makes the arbitrary decision that *if* her breasts stop shaking, "some of the fragments of the afternoon might be collected." It is by "concentrating his attention," not by laying hands on her, that he tries first to still her breasts, and second to make some sense of fragmentary impressions.

The unstable nature of the speaker's sense of identity in "Hysteria" is an extreme case. But if we think of the way in which we show different aspects of ourselves to different people – parents, teachers, friends, bank managers, husbands, lovers, wives – then it is less difficult to comprehend what Eliot meant when he said "a self is an ideal and largely practical construction . . . The self is a construction in space and time." In different situations and with different companions, individuals are capable of being quite different. Is there, then, any such thing as a "real" self?

The waiter in "Hysteria" might also be on the verge of madness.

Prufrock, unlike most of Eliot's voices, has a name by which we identify him. He is very much aware of the discrepancy between the importance of his personal appearance – his morning coat, collar and necktie "rich and modest, but asserted by a simple pin" – and the feelings he has that are not in keeping with the correctness of his dress. He also feels vulnerable and knows, or thinks he knows, that other guests at a social gathering will notice his bald spot and thin arms and legs. These are chinks in his armor. It is as though they imply some inner failing that contradicts the appearance he presents to society.

Prufrock may be hesitant and uncertain, but he is aware of the multiplicity of selves contained within his single person:

> There will be time, there will be time
> To prepare a face to meet the faces that you meet
> There will be time to murder and create.

One way of understanding these lines is to think of how facial expressions or attitudes are adjusted to correspond appropriately to different people and situations. The

"I shall sit here, serving tea to friends" ("Portrait of a Lady").

poetry here imitates the Biblical verses: "A time to kill, and a time to heal; a time to break down, and a time to build up" (Ecclesiastes, III). But the change in rhythm, and the final rhyme of that particular passage in "Prufrock," marks a deliberate contrast from the resonance of the Bible. Instead it echoes the triviality of the popular song "tea for you, and tea for me, tea for two, and you for me." The verse moves from something that sounds wise and significant to the trivial. Both are "true" and seem irreconcilable, even though Eliot has put them together.

The speaker in "Portrait of a Lady" is also aware of such discrepancies. He is deeply embarrassed because the "Lady" of the title has overstepped the bounds of good manners. She has asked him directly why he and she have never become close friends. He comments:

> And I must borrow every changing shape
> To find expression . . . dance, dance
> Dance like a dancing bear,
> Cry like a parrot, chatter like an ape.

Each of the animals he mentions can be trained to imitate human beings in some way. But the lines also imply that humans are animals, too, capable of acquiring good behavior, but remaining fundamentally uncivilized.

The poem "Mr. Apollinax" takes a similar situation – in this case a social gathering of well-bred Americans. There are the inevitable tea cups and polite conversation, but "He is a charming man," with reference to Mr. Apollinax, soon becomes "but after all what did he mean?" and "His pointed ears . . . he must be unbalanced." The other guests are embarrassed and unable to cope with the more primitive presence that has been among them: Mr. Apollinax has refused to suppress uncivilized aspects of his nature in the interests of polite society. Of the other guests, the speaker remembers only trivialities: "a slice of lemon and a bitten macaroon." Mr. Apollinax was

"Mr. Eugenides . . . Asked me in demotic French / To luncheon at the Cannon Street Hotel / Followed by a weekend at the Metropole" (The Waste Land).

uncomfortable company, but memorable.

Civilization, then, is a fragile veneer. Characters in the poems may conspire to bury the unacceptable, but it always breaks through. Aunt Helen in the poem of the same name can impose decorum to a certain extent even after her death: the undertaker wipes his feet before he goes into the house; but though she was a "maiden aunt," she can't deny the instinct that makes the housemaid sit on the footman's knee. Even so, this basic instinct for sexual contact becomes mere impropriety within the terms of the poem – there is no energy or excitement in the encounter. Death itself is somehow neutralized. Instead of being a great or terrifying adventure, or a cause of grief, there is simply silence; an undertaker who "was aware that this sort of thing had occurred before." It is as if Aunt Helen had never been properly alive – or as if she were intent on denying the fact.

Working-class women in 1912. Eliot represented depressed urban scenes in poems such as "Preludes." In "Prufrock" such scenes are contrasted with glittering social occasions.

The notion of social impropriety makes "Hysteria" particularly effective, too. It takes place in a public place and there is something scandalous in the idea of someone going mad, however quietly, while everyone around is well behaved. Prufrock knows he cannot disturb the gathering in the drawing room by asking his "overwhelming question." We infer that it is in the nature of "what is the meaning of life?" and recognize his difficulty. How can the politeness of "toast and tea" in privileged surroundings be reconciled with the other reality of "half deserted streets," of "restless nights in one-night cheap hotels" and "sawdust restaurants"? Both settings can be regarded as aspects of Prufrock himself – "I, the objective world, and my feelings about it, are an indissoluble whole" – the "streets that follow like a tedious argument" and the room "where women come and go/ Talking of Michelangelo" are quite different, but both belong to him and are externalizations of particular states of mind. Prufrock has a third reality: in his imagination he has heard mermaids singing and seen them "riding seaward on the waves." It is in these final images that we glimpse a real sense of his possibilities – but he fails, unable to synthesize his awareness of different feelings and realities. We are left with the sense that modern life is an evasion; trivialities ensure that society is distracted from important or frightening questions.

There are no complete characters in the poems, and the voices that speak do not perceive others as complete, either. Parts of bodies are described: Prufrock has "known the arms" and "known the eyes"; while in the "Preludes" (which despite their title lead to nothing) there are hands, feet and "short square fingers" – in each case they belong to the dreary urban scenes. The second "Prelude" begins:

> The morning comes to consciousness
> Of faint stale smells of beer

The lines seems straightforward until we ask to whom does the "consciousness" belong? The next two lines compound the problem:

> From the saw-dust trampled street
> With all its muddy feet that press
> To early coffee stands.

The muddy feet do not literally belong to the street, but to people in it (people who "belong" to it as their element) who are thus rendered anonymous and depersonalized. The process of fragmentation and dehumanization seems complete in these lines from "Rhapsody on a Windy Night":

> . . . the hand of the child, automatic,
> Slipped out and pocketed a toy . . .
> I could see nothing behind that child's eye.

Eyes are traditionally regarded as windows on the soul, and souls are precisely what are lacking in the nervous self-conscious voices found in *Prufrock and Other Observations*.

Factory workers leaving for home. "His soul stretched tight across the skies / That fade behind a city block, / Or trampled by insistent feet / At four and five and six o'clock" ("Preludes, IV").

3 *The Waste Land*

...the first danger is that of assuming that there must be just one interpretation of the poem as a whole, that must be right... But as for the meaning of the poem as a whole, it is not exhausted by any explanation, for the meaning is what the poem means to different sensitive readers.

(T.S.Eliot, from "The Frontiers of Criticism")

Eliot always refused to explain what a poem or a line in one of his plays meant. He was not being deliberately unhelpful, it was a firmly held belief. The poet, he wrote,

may know the history of [the poem's] composition, the material which has gone in and come out in an unrecognizable form, and he knows what he was trying to do and what he was meaning to mean. But what a poem means is as much what it means to others as what it means to the author; and indeed, in the course of time a poet may become merely a reader in respect of his own works, forgetting his original meaning.

The Waste Land explores many aspects of human experience. It can be analyzed as a meditation on isolation, on the difficulty or impossibility of communication, on boredom, sexual sterility, civilization that has lost its religious faith, or as a search for spirituality, a journey through London and a summary of legend, myth and

Opposite *Eliot signing a copy of his own* Collected Poems.

48

Devastation in Shoreditch, London, caused by a Zeppelin raid in 1915. Such scenes are implied by Eliot's title The Waste Land.

literature through the ages. All of these are at least partly true to the poem's character, but any reading that concentrates on one possibility at the expense of others falsifies and reduces the poem. Eliot's wide range of reference should not discourage readers. Undoubtedly the historical context is important; life in London during and after the First World War must have appeared aimless and

without meaning. Some commentators see Eliot as a social critic; it is, however, a mistake to interpret his work as a platform for reform. His extraordinary and bewildering poetry articulates the ills of modern society, but deliberately yields no answers.

We can claim that *The Waste Land* is about such things because certain images recur throughout – the poet's voice does not point out where the interest lies, readers have to make connections for themselves. For example, the second section of the poem, "A Game of Chess," begins with a description of a highly ornate, artificial and stately room. The language is as formal as the setting it describes. But with no explanation it moves into dialogue, and the poetry suddenly becomes colloquial:

"My nerves are bad tonight. Yes, bad. Stay with me.
. . .
"What is that noise?"
    The wind under the door.
"What is that noise now? What is the wind doing?"

It is likely that one voice is male, the other female, but there is no evidence to confirm this impression – it is also possible that the question and answer take place in the mind of one person. There is always more than one interpretation.

Another change in pace introduces a jazz rhythm:

O O O O that Shakespeherian Rag –
It's so elegant
So intelligent

We infer that for the nervous voices the rag-time provides some variety and distraction – as indeed it does for the readers. But its function is only temporary: the voices return to their restless search for something to take their minds from boredom, which they find in the ritual of "the hot water at ten," a "closed car at four," and a "game of chess."

The third part of "A Game of Chess" is expressed by a working-class voice, telling of a husband back from war:

When Lil's husband got demobbed, I said –
I didn't mince my words, I said to her myself . . .
Now Albert's coming back make yourself a bit smart.

A London Music Hall. Eliot's line "O the moon shone bright on Mrs. Porter / And on her daughter" was a rewriting of a popular song: "O the moon shine bright on Charlie Chaplin, / His boots are crackin' / For want of blackin', / and his little baggy trousers, / They need mendin', / Before they send him / To the Dardanelles."

The voice tells of Lil's false teeth and her abortion. It is interrupted by someone else calling "HURRY UP PLEASE IT'S TIME." This voice, as well as being a landlord of a pub at closing time, is a voice of prophecy, insisting that time is running out for mankind in general.

"A Game of Chess" (unlike the board game) starts with a queen and moves to pawns – the working class – at the

A London Gin Palace in 1921. The working-class voices in "A Game of Chess" belong to a similar setting.

end. The central voices belong to the middle classes: "knights" are reduced to a shell-shocked ex-soldier, who thinks he is still in "rat's alley," suggesting the trenches of the First World War. He is no better off than the aristocracy or the workers: the sickness affecting the modern world respects no class barriers. The "strange synthetic perfumes" of the queen are as artificial as Lil's false teeth;

differences in the movement of the verse and language suggest great divisions between the lives, and yet emptiness and desolation are shown as common to every stratum of society.

One of Eliot's notes directs our attention to Shakespeare's *Antony and Cleopatra*. The opening lines of "A Game of Chess,"

> The Chair she sat in, like a burnished throne,
> Glowed on marble, . . .

The opening of "A Game of Chess" recalls Shakespeare's Cleopatra: "The barge she sat in, like a burnish'd throne, | Burn'd on the water. The poop was beaten gold; | Purple the sails . . ."

are a recollection of Enobarbus's description of Cleopatra:

> The barge she sat in, like a burnish'd throne,
> Burn'd on the water. The poop was beaten gold;
> Purple the sails, and so perfumed that
> The winds were love-sick with them; . . .

> (*Antony and Cleopatra*, II, ii)

At the end of "A Game of Chess" the voices change. "Goonight Bill. Goonight Lou. Goonight May. Goonight./Ta ta," turns into "Goodnight ladies, goodnight, sweet ladies." The working-class farewells move into Ophelia's last words before she drowns herself in Hamlet.

Eliot's notes do not give us sources for all of his references. However, one level of meaning can be found by painstakingly identifying them. If one decides to interpret the poem in this way, Shakespeare would be very important. "A Game of Chess," for example, begins by recalling *Antony and Cleopatra* but moves very rapidly to *Cymbeline*. The description of the "antique mantel" and the richness of the room in general echoes Iachimo's descriptions of Imogen's room (II, iv). Cleopatra and the rape of Philomel are both mentioned in the same passage from *Cymbeline*, which portrays betrayal and doubt. "Those are pearls that were his eyes" is one of many quotations from *The Tempest*; and as Lou and May's "goonight" modulates into a more formal "goodnight, sweet ladies," it is Ophelia's voice from *Hamlet* that we hear – her last words in the play before she drowns herself.

Reading the poem is undoubtedly a different experience if one brings a wide knowledge of literature to it. If we know the stories of Cleopatra, Imogen and Ophelia our reading of *The Waste Land* will be transformed in various ways – as Shakespeare has been transformed into a "Shakespeherian rag" in the poem. But an equally good way of understanding it is to pay close attention to the way the rhythm of the lines changes, or the kind of language that is used, and to compare the movement of one passage with that of the one that precedes or follows it and ask why these dislocations occur. There is never a single correct answer, but there are answers to be found.

The range of Eliot's literary allusion is vast. The title of the first part of *The Waste Land* is taken from "The Order of Service for the Burial of the Dead," which is in the Book of Common Prayer. It provides an inauspicious but accurate opening; people throughout the poem are more dead than alive. The voices seeking distraction in "A Game of Chess" are interested only in passing the time, not in living. One of the voices in "The Burial of the Dead" comments:

A crowd flowed over London Bridge, so many,
I had not thought death had undone so many.

One way of viewing the poem is to consider it as a journey, but one in which the participants have no idea where they are going or why. The purposeful journey of

Chaucer's pilgrims setting out for Canterbury. Eliot evokes the first lines of Chaucer's Canterbury Tales *in "The Burial of the Dead."*

Chaucer's pilgrimage to Canterbury (recalled by the opening of *The Waste Land*) has something in common with medieval quest romances, many of which involve a search. The quest for the Holy Grail, for example, involves a difficult journey across barren countryside that can be regenerated only by some kind of sacrifice – in part the difficulties of the journey itself. The movie *Star Wars* is a perfect example of a modern quest romance: against all the odds a young man and his trusty companions overcome great difficulties and triumph over evil. The hero has moments of doubt, but is sustained by faith even after his elderly mentor is killed.

The Christian religion shares many aspects of more ancient faiths – these are also incorporated into *The Waste Land*. In primitive fertility myths, for example, a young man, a king or god, is slain each year to ensure that winter passes and the crops grow again. Similarly, Christ spent forty days in the wilderness (or wasteland) to prepare for a final sacrifice on behalf of mankind. The Fisher King who appears in Eliot's poem is unable to die, and so his lands remain barren, like the streets of London depicted in *The Waste Land*. It is not specifically Christianity that is missing, but any kind of religious faith. In "The Burial of the Dead" someone consults a clairvoyant, Madame Sosostris, who is "known to be the wisest woman in Europe," but there is nothing about her that inspires faith. She seems only too human, not least because she has "a bad cold." Religion is redundant and has been replaced with superstition.

In The Waste Land *clairvoyance and fortune-telling have become substitutes for religion.*

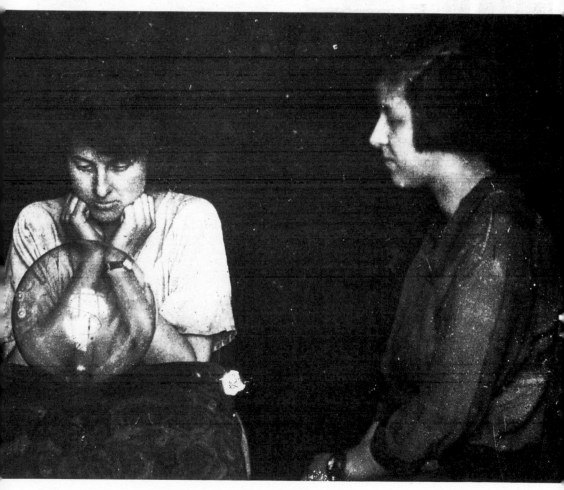

Andrew Marvell, Esq.

There is no rain:

> ...the sun beats,
> and the dead tree gives no shelter, the cricket no relief,
> And the dry stone no sound of water.

The land and its people are sterile. There are many sexual encounters in the poem, but they all lack love, tenderness or even energy. The house agent's clerk and the typist in "The Fire Sermon" are the most obvious example:

> Flushed and decided, he assaults at once;
> Exploring hands encounter no defence;
> His vanity requires no response,
> And makes a welcome of indifference.

To reflect the nature of the modern world, there is no traditional hero in the poem and no sustained narrative. We are presented with "a heap of broken images." In the notes, Eliot suggests that Tiresias (who observes the typist's encounter with the clerk) is the most important person in the poem, and that it is he who unites all the others. This can be established only after detailed reading and is not particularly convincing even then. The reader's initial impression is more likely to be of countless different voices, none of which has preeminent authority.

Characters in the poem are unable to find their own words. Their feelings are not new, or unique, they can only express themselves in "borrowed" language. In "The Fire Sermon," for example, Eliot imitates Andrew Marvell's poem "To His Coy Mistress," written in the seventeenth century. Marvell's lines read, "But at my back I always hear / Time's wingéd chariot hurrying near." These lines appear at a point in his poem where an argument has been established – he is trying to talk the woman he loves into bed – and the moment has come to press the point home. Time is running out, because she will not be young and beautiful forever. In "The Fire Sermon" the lines are referred to twice: "But at my back in a cold blast I hear/ The rattle of bones, and a chuckle spread from ear to ear." A little later, they reappear slightly differently:

> But at my back from time to time I hear
> The sound of horns and motors, which shall bring
> Sweeney to Mrs. Porter in the spring.

Opposite *Lines from Andrew Marvell's poem "To His Coy Mistress" are transformed in "The Fire Sermon" section of* The Waste Land.

Marvell's witty and elegant verse cannot be sustained; it breaks down into the rewriting of a popular music hall song: "O the moon shine bright on Mrs. Porter/And on her daughter." The overall impression, then, is of characters who lack cohesion, who are merely scraps from different ages. The intention is to show that of all the styles imitated in *The Waste Land* none has any more authority than another. Although there are different techniques of writing, none has a monopoly on truth or reality.

The opening of the poem, with its references to spring and rebirth – which the speaker resists – prepares for all of these themes to be developed. So we need to ask what, if anything, has been achieved by the end of the poem. Eliot himself resisted drawing any conclusions. Earlier, in "The Fire Sermon," one character has been "fishing in the dull canal . . . round behind the gashouse." In the last lines a speaker sits "upon the shore/Fishing, with the arid plain behind me," which suggests that the wasteland has been crossed. He fishes in the sea rather than a man-made canal, but it does not seem to be an illuminating experience.

An audience being entertained at a music hall.

64

The whole poem is constructed using fragments of verse that do not fit comfortably together. This fragmentation becomes even more extreme in the last paragraph. It consists of a question, a line from a nursery rhyme, a line of medieval Italian, half a line of nineteenth-century French, some Jacobean English, and it ends in Sanskrit. It is perfectly valid, then, to conclude that this muddle and confusion is intended to be like the tower of Babel: Eliot does not expect us to be linguists and we are meant to see the ending as a complete failure of communication – we are not meant to understand what is going on. Even if we are told that "Datta," "Dayadhvam" and "Damyata" translate as Give, Sympathize and Control, and that "Shantih" is best translated as "the peace that passeth all understanding" – we may still not be convinced that this muddle of sounds conveys a sense of peace. It may be written in a foreign language simply because that language, like the peace it evokes, is forever alien to the wasteland. The form of words and their actual meaning contradict each other. Another interpretation, however, might suggest that "Shantih, shantih, shantih" is an optimistic conclusion; certainly the repetition of these words produces a peaceful sound. Each interpretation contains some truth; none of them tells the whole story. It is up to the reader to sift through the "fragments" again and again, adjusting and re-adjusting ideas about the poem with each successive reading.

Opposite *View of the London skyline from the Monument, facing St. Paul's Cathedral, 1927.*

4 *Four Quartets*

Eliot was baptized into the Anglican faith in 1927, and in subtle ways his poetry began to change from that time. At first sight, the poems that make up the *Four Quartets* are almost as difficult as *The Waste Land*, but whereas one can argue endlessly as to whether *The Waste Land* has any underlying coherence, there is no doubt that the later poem has. The pattern is intended, not accidental, and is fundamental to Eliot's new belief that the lives of human beings may seem empty and meaningless, but that there is a higher authority – God. Daily life may still seem chaotic and confused, but faith in eternity gives meaning to life and a pattern to the poetry.

Different states of mind are dramatized in *Four Quartets*, but unlike *The Waste Land*, these all belong to the same person, and for the first time Eliot speaks in his own voice. Moments of doubt and confusion are still present, but ultimately they are incorporated into the structure of the poem.

"Burnt Norton" begins with a complex meditation on time; but as always it is the poetry that is important. In the first five lines, the word "Time" is repeated on seven occasions. This insistence conveys one of the central paradoxes of the poem: how can anyone imagine eternity when everything we experience happens within temporal boundaries? The repetition of "time" gives the reader a sense of being trapped, which expresses the paradox, even if he or she fails to follow the philosophy behind the lines.

Throughout the *Four Quartets* such passages of abstract thought are illustrated by examples. In "Burnt Norton" the abstract idea is highlighted by the description of a moment of sudden understanding that happens in a rose garden. In the Prufrock volume there are few images of nature, and these are always corrupted. The woman in "Portrait of a Lady" holds a lilac – a symbol of spring and rebirth – but significantly she twists it in her fingers, as though she is denying life. Urban settings and closed interiors characterized the early poems and *The Waste Land*, but with the rose garden image in "Burnt Norton" Eliot introduces symbols of fertility. This is an indication of a more hopeful state of mind.

Eliot sitting at his typewriter.

This particular garden has associations with the Garden of Eden, "our first world," but it is also an actual place that Eliot visited, a formal cultivated garden dating from the eighteenth century. Through mythological associations, then, it evokes Adam and Eve in Eden before the Fall. But because it is a real location it also represents time-bound mortal existence. These two associations fuse, creating the perfect background for the glimpse of eternity that the poet has when he looks into the "dry concrete, brown edged pool" and suddenly sees it "filled with water out of sunlight." The mystical experience is elusive, but the transformation is evidence of something supernatural – or divine – interacting with the ordinary world. It is fleeting: "a cloud passed, and the pool was empty," but the poem asks us to believe that the illusion of the dry pool filled with water is more real than the fact:

Go, go, go, said the bird: human kind
Cannot bear very much reality.

Opposite *The Garden of Eden is one association evoked by the rose garden in "Burnt Norton": "Other echoes/Inhabit the garden. Shall we follow?"*

Moments of revelation and understanding like these are glimpses of the reality of eternity – which by its very nature is normally hidden from mankind.

The second part of "Burnt Norton" is about pattern and repetition in the universe. Within the poem, the circulation of the blood in each individual becomes an imitation of the movement of the planets; the boarhound chasing the boar mimics the constellations in the skies. Everything fits into the eternal plan, and the lyrical regularity of the poetry in this passage imitates the pattern. There is no punctuation at the end of the lines to separate the thought that moves from the sky, to trees, to the earth and back to the stars again.

The third part of "Burnt Norton," however, takes us back to urban settings familiar to us from *The Waste Land*:

Here is a place of disaffection
Time before and time after
In a dim light ...

The verse describes "strained time-ridden faces," men who are no more than "bits of paper" blown aimlessly by the wind in London suburbs, their lives empty and meaningless. Eliot's honesty compels him to admit that faith is not easy, and the fourth part of "Burnt Norton" questions the experience in the rose garden. Sunlight produced the illusion/reality of water in the pool until a cloud passed over. Here, "the black cloud carries the sun away" and a series of questions follows, expressing moments of doubt. The rhythm of the lines falls away:

London suburbs, like this one, form an important part of the background to the Four Quartets.

Will the sunflower turn to us, will the clematis
Stray down, bend to us; tendril and spray
Clutch and cling?
Chill
Fingers of Yew be curled
Down on us?

The sunflower and clematis are positive images, the sunflower particularly associated with Christ. The yew, on the other hand, is a dark tree usually associated with death and burial. In the last two lines of the passage, however, a regular verse movement is re-established as confirmation of faith:

Clipped yew trees in a churchyard: gloomy trees often associated with death and burial.

      . . . After the kingfisher's wing
Has answered light to light, and is silent, the light is still
At the still point of the turning world.

As with the sunflower, the kingfisher is traditionally an emblem of Christ. Its wing reflects the light, recalling the "heart of light" in the rose garden.

To speak of eternity in terms of a "fleeting moment" is a paradox, because however brief a "moment" might be, it is still a measurement in time. It is, however, all that is available to us. Feeling and intuition have to be translated into words if they are going to be communicated, but the task is not an easy one. The difficulty of writing is one that Eliot raises more than once in the *Four Quartets*. In the last part of "Burnt Norton" he says:

> Words strain,
> Crack and sometimes break, under the burden,
> Under the tension, slip, slide, perish,
> Decay with imprecision, will not stay in place,
> Will not stay still.

Language is a problem that occupies him again in "East Coke": "the intolerable wrestle/With words and meanings." The struggle is integrated into the poem and has been mastered by the end. Similarly, the moment in the rose garden is followed by doubt, but affirmed at the end of "Little Gidding." The *Four Quartets* are an attempt to reconcile inconsistencies, not to pretend that they do not exist. The title's musical associations suggest the harmony that is ultimately achieved in the poetry.

The "Burnt" of "Burnt Norton" signifies destruction – the building was named after the original house that stood on the site. It was destroyed by fire, an indication of the transient nature of the works of men. But "burnt" becomes a different kind of fire at the end of "Little Gidding," the last poem in the sequence. Here, instead of destroying, fire cleanses and renews. But even as we read the very last lines, "the fire and the rose are one," we are intended to recall Burnt Norton, as well as the rose garden, and recognize that they both stand for necessary stages on the way to the eternity.

Although it was not originally intended to follow "Burnt Norton," "East Coker" begins with a reflection on the earlier poem:

> Houses rise and fall, crumble, are extended,
> Are removed, destroyed, restored, or in their place
> Is an open field, or a factory, or a by-pass.

What characterizes the history of life on earth is continual change. The imitation of Ecclesiastes in the first part is rather different from its appearance in "Prufrock," but the allusion ensures that the word "time" continues to chime in the reader's ear:

> The time of the seasons and the constellations
> The time of milking and the time of harvest
> The time of the coupling of man and woman . . .

Eliot imagines medieval country people in an open field in East Coker. The image is assisted by the use of Chaucerian English: "daunsinge" and "matrimonie," for example. The last words of the passage, "Dung and death," equate them with "Old fire to ashes, and ashes to earth" from the beginning of the poem – but also indicate

a different kind of endurance, the cycle of seasons, and birth following death.

Each of the poems in the sequence has an element associated with it. In "Burnt Norton" the dominant element is fire, in "East Coker" it is earth, water in "The Dry Salvages," while in "Little Gidding" it is air. But just as the place names that give each poem its title are really only starting points, the fire, earth, water and air are not obtrusive; they form part of the overall pattern. Fire, for instance, is almost equally important in "Little Gidding," while the end of "East Coker":

> The wave cry, the wind cry, the vast waters
> Of the petrel and the porpoise . . .

anticipates the beginning of "The Dry Salvages," which describes the Mississippi River and the ocean.

Steamboats on the Mississippi River. "I think that the river / Is a strong brown god – sullen, untamed and intractable . . . . Useful, but untrustworthy as a conveyor of commerce . . . " ("The Dry Salvages").

Eliot aged twelve at Eastern Point. Images from his childhood vacations are used in Four Quartets.

East Coker and the Dry Salvages had a private significance for Eliot. His family originally came from the Somerset village of East Coker, while the Dry Salvages were part of the scenery of childhood vacations. Family history and personal history are both ways of thinking about time – the constant preoccupation of the poems – but "Little Gidding" replaces private significance with a wider view, that of English history. Little Gidding is a

The church at East Coker where Eliot's ashes are buried. His ancestors came from the Somerset village.

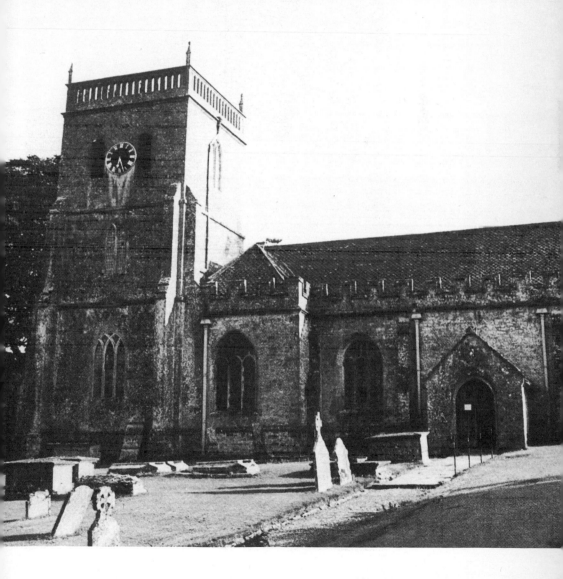

The poet John Donne (1573 – 1631) who donated a silver chalice to the church at Little Gidding.

village near Huntingdon that has strong religious and historical associations. It also has literary links: the Elizabethan poets John Donne and George Herbert both visited the religious community that Nicholas Ferrar founded there in 1625. King Charles found brief refuge there after his defeat at the Battle of Naseby in 1646, and because of the community's allegiance to the King, the chapel was destroyed by Cromwell's troops the following year. The line "If you came at night like a broken king" refers to Charles, while "the tombstone" is that of Nicholas Ferrar.

Eliot's use of the name "Little Gidding" sums up a

particular period in English history, but in the second part of the poem he alludes to the time at which he was writing. Although he does not mention the Second World War directly (any more than he mentioned the First World War in *The Waste Land*), he refers to bombing raids on London:

> Ash on an old man's sleeve
> Is all the ash the burnt roses leave.
> Dust in the air suspended
> Marks the place where a story ended.
> Dust inbreathed was a house –

"Inbreathed" implies a vision of the house imploding and also makes the experience personal to the observer: dust inbreathed, or inhaled, was once part of a house. The "dark dove with the flickering tongue" in the same section refers to an enemy bomber plane. These references are obvious once they have been pointed out, but they are sufficiently unspecific to also suggest general destruction. In this way, Eliot fuses contemporary history with past conflict. The destruction of Little Gidding becomes part of a pattern into which the Second World War fits.

Very deliberately, Eliot's language invokes precisely the opposite of what he describes. The ash left by the "burnt roses" is an imaginative way of describing a fiery red explosion. But within the context of the poem it also recalls "Burnt Norton" and the rose garden, which suggest belief in an ultimate reconciliation of man with the Divine. In the same way, the dark dove with the "flickering tongue" causes death and destruction, but it also makes readers remember the opposite: the Holy Ghost is frequently described as a dove, though never a "dark" one, and in the New Testament it descended on the disciples with tongues of pentecostal fire.

This contradiction is vital to the poem's meaning. Section four of "Little Gidding" begins with a rewriting of the earlier "dark dove" passage:

> The dove descending breaks the air
> With flame of incandescent terror
> Of which the tongues declare
> The one discharge from sin and error.
> The only hope, or else despair
>   Lies in the choice of pyre or pyre –
>   To be redeemed from fire by fire.

This time it is the Holy Ghost, not a hostile bomber, but it is no less frightening, though it inspires a different kind of terror. The distinction is that by accepting divine "fire" – the life of struggle that faith implies – ultimately peace will be found. Eliot uses the same word to mean two different things. When he says "To be redeemed from fire by fire," the first usage implies destruction; the second fire represents a cleansing process, divesting oneself of the love of earthly things. Eliot recognizes that this is difficult and painful but believes it is the only way of attaining Divine grace and eternity.

Opposite *The Holy Ghost descends on the disciples as tongues of fire.*

A German bomber plane. " . . . the dark dove with the flickering tongue" ("Little Gidding").

Similar paradoxes are implied in "East Coker," where the poet says:

> . . . wait without hope
> For hope would be hope for the wrong thing; wait
> without love
> For love would be love of the wrong thing.

The realization of these sentiments is necessary to free oneself from "Attachment to self and to things and to persons," as he says in "Little Gidding."

The images, substance and rhythm of the *Four Quartets* explore universal problems. Read in sequence, the components of each poem begin to come together; conflicts are reconciled, and the completed structure becomes an expression of deeply-held belief.

5 *Murder in the Cathedral*

When *Murder in the Cathedral* was first performed in June 1935, one reviewer felt that "it may well mark a turning point in English drama." Successful and popular plays of the period were written in prose. *Murder in the Cathedral*, however, was both successful and popular, in spite of the fact that, like all of Eliot's plays, it is written in verse.

The play owed much of its "newness," including the poetry, to Eliot's return to the very beginnings of drama. Whether he was writing poetry or plays, he was always aware of literary tradition. Ancient Greek tragedy had its roots in religion; E. Martin Browne says it was written and performed "to celebrate the cult associated with a sacred spot by displaying the story of its origin." This was precisely the task that Eliot had undertaken when he agreed to write a play for Canterbury Cathedral. After the martyrdom of Thomas à Becket, his tomb in the Cathedral became a shrine for pilgrims who traveled from all over Europe during the Middle Ages. The stark formality of Eliot's verse and the play's lack of action are highly appropriate, too, as both aspects belong to the Classical Greek tradition.

In *Murder in the Cathedral*, as in Greek tragedy, language conveys most of the action. The Chorus of Women of Canterbury and the three Priests "fill in" the historical events leading to Becket"s return to England; similarly we do not see Becket's interview with the King; it is reported

Eliot at a rehearsal of Murder in the Cathedral.

by a Messenger. This helps to focus attention on Thomas's mind, the real center of the play's action.

Medieval English drama, like Ancient Greek drama, had its origins in religious services. The Church's Litany – where the priest speaks and is answered by the congregation – provides a dialogue from which the Medieval Mystery Plays developed. These always had religious subject matter. Eliot, then, combines traditions from two cultures and makes of them something new.

Sense of place was always important to him: London in *The Waste Land* and the locations of the *Four Quartets* are obvious examples. So the significance of writing a play about Thomas à Becket's murder, which would be performed in the place where it actually happened, did not escape him.

Opposite *Becket's tomb in Canterbury Cathedral.*

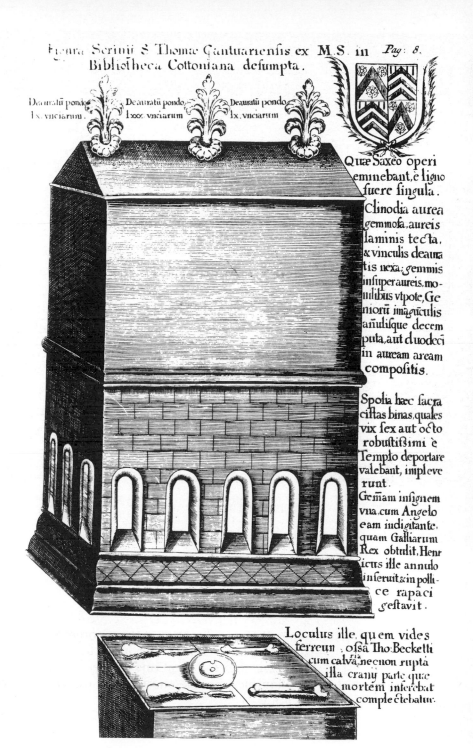

Figura Scrinii S Thomæ Cantuariensis ex M.S. in Bibliotheca Cottoniana desumpta.

Deauratū pondo lx. vnciarum.

Deauratū pondo lxxx. vnciarum

Deauratū pondo lx. vnciarum

Quæ Saxeo operi eminebant, è ligno fuere singula.

Clinodia aurea gemmosa, aureis laminis tecta, & vinculis deauratis nexa; gemmis insuper aureis, monilibus vtpote, Geniorū imagunculis anulisque decem puta, aut duodeci in auream aream compositis.

Spolia hæc sacra cistas binas, quales vix sex aut octo robustissimi è Templo deportare valebant, impleverunt. Gemmam insignem vna, cum Angelo eam indigitante, quam Galliarum Rex obtulit, Henricus ille annulo inseruit & in pollice rapaci gestavit.

Loculus ille, quem vides ferreun, ossa Tho Becketti cum calva, necnon rupta illa cranij parte quæ mortem inferebat complectebatur.

The historical background to the play is important, but can be summarized briefly. Thomas à Becket (1118–70) was a merchant's son who became a powerful statesman. He helped Henry II restore order to England after a period of civil war. Henry had great confidence in Becket's abilities and made him Chancellor of England. He later made him the Archbishop of Canterbury, Head of the Church in England. But at this point, against Henry's wishes, Becket resigned the Chancellorship. In his opinion it was not possible to serve the interests of both Church and State. He and Henry quarreled over various issues, and eventually Becket fled to France, where he remained in exile for seven years. He returned to Canterbury in December 1170. This is where Eliot's play begins. Becket was aware that his life was in danger, but he was

Henry II and Becket almost come to blows.

Opposite *Eliot's play has its roots in the tradition of the Medieval Mystery Play.*

determined to preach a sermon on Christmas day in his own Cathedral. He was murdered by four of the King's knights four days later.

Murder in the Cathedral includes Eliot's version of Becket's Christmas morning sermon. This must have had a powerful effect on audiences watching the first performance of the play in the Cathedral itself. It is as though they become a congregation rather than an audience. This is one of the ways in which Eliot gives a sense of immediacy to his historical subject matter.

Murder in the Cathedral opens with a Chorus – another element taken from Greek drama. The Women of Canterbury expect and are anxious about their

Archbishop's return, "it would not be well." Life has been neither wholly good nor wholly bad since he went away, but they have at least known what to expect:

> We have suffered various oppression,
> But mostly we are left to our own devices,
> And we are content if we are left alone.

Their fearfulness conveys a strong sense of doom. Three Priests discuss the situation, then a Messenger enters and announces that Becket has returned:

> . . . in pride and sorrow, affirming all his claims,
> Assured, beyond doubt, of the devotion of the people.

Scene from the Life of St. Thomas. Becket excommunicates the Bishops who had taken King Henry's side against him and the Church.

The murder of Becket in the Cathedral.

But the Messenger is not optimistic about relations between Becket and the King: their peace is a "patched up affair." The gathering sense of disquiet is voiced by the Chorus:

> You come with applause, you come rejoicing; but you
> come bringing death into Canterbury:
> A doom on the house, a doom on yourself, a doom on
>   the world.
>
> We do not wish anything to happen.

When Thomas appears he does not put their fears to rest, but tells them that whatever happens is inevitable.

This is the crux of the matter. Though Thomas is a man of stature and integrity, his murder is not, in the play's terms, a tragedy. Instead, it is cause for the Church to celebrate. Before he is killed, Thomas reaches the same state of grace that the *Four Quartets* advocate: he has divested himself of love for all earthly things. In his martyrdom he becomes an example for the rest of mankind.

But he has not yet reached this state when he first returns to the Cathedral. He has to confront and overcome a number of difficulties. The conflict in his mind is dramatized through his dialogue with four Tempters. Thomas refers to his trial by temptation as "strife with shadows" – a point eloquently illustrated when the play was televised in 1936. Each of the Tempters in turn was superimposed onto an image of Becket on the screen. The parts of the Four Tempters and the Four Knights are usually played by the same actors. Although the Priests and the Chorus are present on the stage when Becket confronts both groups, they witness only the action of the Knights – the struggle with temptation is a mental one.

The First Tempter addresses Becket as "Old Tom, gay Tom, Becket of London" and reminds him of his youth. Becket dismisses him with the words "you come twenty years too late." The Second Tempter tries to persuade him that resigning the Chancellorship was a grave error and that by resuming the cares of State he could use his power to benefit the people. His dialogue with Becket ironically echoes the statement and response of priest and people in church services: they have half a line each. Power, the Second Tempter tells him, "is present for him who will wield":

> THOMAS
> Who shall have it?
> > TEMPTER
> > He who will come.
> THOMAS
> What shall be the month?
> > TEMPTER
> > The last from the first.
> THOMAS
> What shall we give it?
> > TEMPTER
> > Pretence of priestly power.
> THOMAS
> Why should we give it?
> > TEMPTER
> > For the power and the glory.

The shock of hearing this phrase, taken from the Lord's Prayer, enables Thomas to exclaim "No!" The words have been taken out of context and their significance twisted: the line should read *"Thine"* – meaning God's – "is the Kingdom, the Power and the Glory."

The Third Tempter is a "rough straightforward Englishman" who wants Thomas to assert the supremacy of the Church over the King. But he is banished when Thomas declares, "no one shall say that I betrayed a king."

Becket expected only three tempters and is unprepared for a fourth. The last temptation is the most difficult and dangerous, for it involves the sin of pride:

> . . . think, Thomas, think of glory after death.
> When the king is dead, there's another king . . .

Although "King is forgotten, when another shall come," "Saint and Martyr rule from the tomb." Thomas admits that he has indeed imagined pilgrims standing in line to pray to him for miracles, but he also knows that such thoughts are his "soul's sickness." He is aware that martyrdom for the wrong reasons can lead only to damnation.

The chorus urges him to "save yourself that we may be saved" – an appeal similar to that of the Second Tempter. But having confronted the Tempters, Becket is resolved on his course of action – or inaction. Addressing Priests, Chorus and audience, he says:

> I know
> What yet remains to show you of my history
> Will seem to most of you at best futility,
> Senseless self-slaughter of a lunatic,
> Arrogant passion of a fanatic

But the sermon that follows the first act, the "Interlude," goes a long way to explaining the Christian view of martyrdom. It is never an accident and never the result of human choice: the true martyr "has lost his will in the will of God . . . and no longer desires anything for himself, not even the glory of being a martyr." The Church on earth may mourn, but it must also rejoice at such a death.

In the second part of the play the Four Knights appear. They charge Thomas with betraying Henry's trust, causing trouble between Henry and the King of France, and between Henry and the Pope, as well as excommunicating three Archbishops who had acted according to Henry's wishes. They leave, but promise to return. Priest and Chorus urge Thomas to lock the doors of the Cathedral, but he refuses to turn it into a "fortress." He is "not in danger, only near to death."

Opposite *Eliot in 1948.*

95

The Knights do return and kill him, but the visual spectacle this presents is subordinate to the Chorus's expression of universal desolation. We have been expecting Becket's death throughout the play; the real dramatic tension comes in the poetry:

> Clean the air! clean the sky! wash the wind! take the stone from the stone, take the skin from the arm, take the muscle from the bone, and wash them.

The mood of emotional intensity that the Chorus generates changes abruptly when the First Knight comes to the front of the stage and addresses the audience directly. In stark contrast to the language of the Chorus, the Knights speak in modern, colloquial English. The effect is both shocking and comic:

> When you come to the point, it does go against the grain to kill an Archbishop . . . So if we seemed a bit rowdy, you will understand why it was, and for my part I am awfully sorry about it.

Opposite
*Canterbury
Cathedral.*

*The Four Knights
murder Becket:
"When you come to
the point, it does go
against the grain to
kill an Archbishop . . .
for my part I am
awfully sorry about
it" (Murder in the
Cathedral).*

Eliot explaining his play with the aid of diagrams, at Princeton University.

With subtle, persuasive arguments, they attempt to justify their action. The Fourth Knight suggests that Becket suffered from some kind of mental disorder and provoked them to kill him. "I think," he tells the audience, "with these facts before you, you will unhesitatingly render a verdict of Suicide while of Unsound Mind." By allowing the Knights to make excuses, Eliot invites audiences to reconsider Becket's motives and make up their own minds about the sacrifice he made. The play is not just a piece of historical drama – although we can read it in that way. For Eliot it expressed an act of faith, which should be considered whatever age we live in.

After their unseemly disruption the Knights leave, and the Priests re-establish a sense of peaceful order. The Church is not "bereft, alone, desolated" by Becket's death, as the First Priest believes to begin with. It has been strengthened by the martyrdom. The Priests offer thanks to God, "who has given us another Saint in Canterbury," and the Chorus closes the play in a different spirit from the way in which they opened it.

Eliot's later plays have contemporary settings but, like *Murder in the Cathedral*, they are all verse dramas. "The first and perhaps the only law of the drama," Eliot said, "is to get the attention of the audience and to keep it."

Epstein's bust of T.S. Eliot.

Glossary

Aiken, Conrad 1889–1973. American novelist and poet.

Babbitt, Irving 1865–1933. American philosopher.

Bergson, Henri 1859–1941. Influential philosopher of the 1920s and 1930s.

Bradley, F.H. 1846–1924. British philosopher. Fellow of Merton College, Oxford, while Eliot was writing his thesis there.

Brooke, Rupert 1887–1915. Brooke, unlike Eliot, was a "traditional" poet; his sonnets written during the First World War are patriotic and do not confront the horror of warfare.

Browning, Robert 1812–89. Victorian poet who wrote a number of dramatic monologues ("My Last Duchess," "The Bishop Orders His Tomb," for example).

Donne, John 1572–1631. Elizabethan poet and Dean of Saint Paul's Cathedral.

Dramatic monologue A character is created by the poet, and the poem is written as though that character (not the poet) is speaking directly to the reader.

Joyce, James 1882–1941. Like Eliot and Virginia Woolf, Joyce was a modernist writer. He wrote prose, not poetry, but his use of myth, fragmentation and repeated images, together with a lack of plot or strong sense of story, indicate that he had much in common with Eliot. His major works are *Dubliners* (1914), *A Portrait of the Artist as a Young Man* (1916), *Ulysses* (1922) and *Finnegan's Wake* (1939).

Herbert, George 1593–1633. Religious poet. Like John Donne, he is now known as one of the "Metaphysical Poets."

Holy Grail The cup used by Christ at the Last Supper. It was this that knights set out to find in their lengthy quests. There are many versions of the Grail Legends; Sir Thomas Malory's fifteenth-century *Morte D'Arthur* includes a quest for the Holy Grail. Eliot refers to later versions: the sonnet "Parsifal" by Paul Verlaine (1844–96) in "The Fire Sermon," as well as Wagner's opera of the same name.

Laforgue, Jules 1860–87. French poet. Eliot said, "The form in which I began to write, in 1908 or 1909, was directly drawn from the study of Laforgue together with the later Elizabethan drama."

Lewis, Percy Wyndham 1882–1957. Novelist, philosopher, poet, critic, editor and artist.

Meter The rhythm of a line of poetry.

Modernism A movement among writers and painters during 1910–1925. The modernists rejected traditional styles and subjects, determined to "make it new."

Mystery Plays Series of short plays illustrating Biblical stories, performed on the same day. Chester, Wakefield, and York cycles of mystery plays are still in existence.

Pound, Ezra 1885–1972. Pound described his endeavors accurately in *Make It New*: "Let it stand that from 1912 onward for a decade and more I was instrumental in forcing into print, and *secondarily* in commenting on, certain work now recognized as valid by all competent readers."

Temporal boundaries Any measurement of the passage of time: a second, a week, a month, a decade, and so on.

Unitarian A religion whose followers believe in one God, irrespective of race or creed.

Woolf, Virginia 1882–1941. Modernist novelist (see James Joyce above). Married to Leonard Woolf, who was also a writer.

List of Dates

1888	Thomas Stearns Eliot born on September 26, in St. Louis, Missouri.
1898	Attends Smith Academy in St. Louis.
1905	Attends Milton Academy near Boston.
1906	Attends Harvard University.
1910	The first two poems of "Preludes" written. To Paris in October to study French literary criticism and philosophy. Eliot also visits London and Munich while in Europe.
1911	Returns to Harvard to continue postgraduate study.
1913	Teaching assistant in the Department of Philosophy at Harvard.
1914	Scholarship to Merton College, Oxford, to complete Ph.D. thesis on F.H. Bradley. Travels through Belgium, Italy and Germany before going to London. Meets Ezra Pound, Conrad Aiken and Wyndham Lewis.
1915	Marries Vivien Haigh-Wood at Hampstead Register Office on June 26. Returns briefly to St. Louis to visit his parents. Starts teaching – first at High Wycombe Grammar School then at Highgate Junior School.
1916	Submits thesis to Harvard. Gives up teaching at the end of the year.

1917	Starts work at Lloyds Bank in the City of London. *Prufrock and Other Observations* published; starts work as assistant editor for the *Egoist*.
1919	"Tradition and the Individual Talent" published in the *Egoist*.
1920	Meets James Joyce in Paris.
1922	*The Waste Land* published in *Criterion*.
1923	*The Waste Land* appears in book form, with notes, published by Leonard and Virginia Woolf's Hogarth Press.
1924	Working on an unfinished play called *Sweeney Agonistes* (fragments of the work can be found in *Collected Poems*).
1925	Leaves the bank to start work for the publishing house Faber and Gwyer.
1927	Is received into the Church of England in June, at Finstock Church in the Cotswolds. "Journey of the Magi" published. Becomes a British citizen in November.
1931	Contracts to publish Joyce's *Finnegan's Wake* in his capacity as editor at Faber and Gwyer.
1932	Gives a series of radio talks on "The Moral Dilemma." Accepts Charles Eliot Norton professorship at Harvard for the academic year. Sails to U.S. on September 17.
1933	Returns to England and is legally separated from his wife. To Paris in November to discuss a new edition of *Ulysses* with James Joyce.
1934	*The Rock* performed at Sadler's Wells in London. Visits Burnt Norton.

1935	*Murder in the Cathedral* performed at Canterbury Cathedral.
1936	*Murder in the Cathedral* televised by the BBC. Eliot visits Little Gidding.
1937	Visits East Coker in August. Travels widely in following years giving lectures.
1938	*Essays Ancient and Modern* – a collection of Eliot's literary criticism – published. *Collected Poems 1909–1935* appears, including the first publication of "Burnt Norton."
1939	*The Family Reunion* opens at Westminster Theatre in March. *Old Possum's Book of Practical Cats* published.
1940	"East Coker" published in *New English Weekly*.
1941	"Dry Salvages" published in *New English Weekly*.
1942	"Little Gidding" published in *New English Weekly*.
1944	*Four Quartets* appear in book form.
1947	Vivien dies unexpectedly at age of 58.
1948	Order of Merit awarded by King George VI in January. Eliot receives Nobel Prize for Literature in November. Valerie Fletcher becomes his secretary.
1953	*The Confidential Clerk* first performed at the Lyceum in August.
1957	Marries Valerie Fletcher on January 10.
1958	*The Elder Statesman* first performed. Eliot's health poor, he and his wife spend winter months in the West Indies during the following years.

| 1965 | Eliot dies on January 4. His ashes taken to St. Michael's Church in East Coker. |

List of Works

Complete Poems and Plays (Faber & Faber, (1969), 1987)

Poetry
Collected Poems 1909–1962 (Faber & Faber, 1974)
The Waste Land: a facsimile and transcript of the original drafts, edited by Valerie Eliot (Faber & Faber, 1971)
Old Possum's Book of Practical Cats (verse for children), (Faber & Faber, (1939), 1989)

Plays
Murder in the Cathedral (Faber & Faber, (1935), 1987)
The Family Reunion (Faber & Faber, (1939), 1988)
The Cocktail Party (Faber & Faber, (1950), 1982)
The Confidential Clerk (Faber & Faber, (1954), 1979)
The Elder Statesman (Faber & Faber, (1958), 1986)

Literary Criticism
Selected Prose of T.S.Eliot, edited with an introduction by Frank Kermode (Faber & Faber, 1975). This includes Eliot's influential essay "Tradition and the Individual Talent" (1919), as well as essays on the Metaphysical Poets, Andrew Marvell, Milton, Yeats, and James Joyce's *Ulysses*. *Essay On Poetry and Poets*, (Faber & Faber, (1957), 1986)

Letters of T.S.Eliot, vol.I 1898 – 1922, edited by Valerie Eliot (Faber & Faber, 1988)

Further Reading

Peter Ackroyd's biography, listed below, is the best full-length biography. E. Martin Browne's book (see below) records his collaboration with Eliot on the staging of his plays, from *Murder in the Cathedral* to *The Elder Statesman*.

ACKROYD, PETER *T.S.Eliot* (Sphere Books, 1984)

BERGONZI, BERNARD *T.S.Eliot* (Macmillan, 1975)

BERGONZI, BERNARD (ed.) *Four Quartets* (Casebook Series, Macmillan, (1968) 1988)

BROWNE, E. MARTIN *The Making of T.S.Eliot's Plays* (Cambridge University Press, 1969)

CLARK, D.R. (ed.) *Twentieth Century Interpretations of Murder in the Cathedral* (Prentice Hall, 1971)

COX, C.B. and ARNOLD P. HINCHLIFFE *The Waste Land* (Casebook Series, Macmillan, (1968) 1988)

GORDON, LYNDALL *Eliot's Early Years* (Oxford University Press, 1988)

HINCHLIFFE, ARNOLD P. (ed.) *T.S.Eliot's Plays* (Casebook Series, Macmillan, 1985)

KENNER, HUGH *The Invisible Poet*: *T.S.Eliot* (W.H.Allen, 1960)

SOUTHAM, C. (ed.) *Prufrock, Gerontion, Ash Wednesday and Other Shorter Poems* (Casebook Series, Macmillan, (1978) 1987)

TRAVERSI, D. *T.S.Eliot, the Longer Poems* (Bodley Head, 1976)

Index

Acknowledgments

The author and publishers would like to thank the following for allowing their illustrations to be reproduced in this book: The Bettmann Archive 25; Mary Evans Picture Library 12, 20, 23, 32, 33, 35, 38, 41, 54, 56, 57, 60, 61, 62, 64, 65, 66, 70, 80, 87, 89, 94, 96, 97; Hulton Picture Company 50, 69, 86, 98; The Rev. David Hunt, East Coker Vicarage 28, 79; The Billie Love Collection 36, 40, 42, 44, 45, 47, 52, 72, 73; The Mansell Collection 15, 16, 18, 22, 31, 59, 82, 88, 90, 92; The Missouri Historical Society 8, 9, 10, 11, 13, 74, 76, 78; Topham Picture Library 7, 26, 29, 49, 83, 99.